# Passive Income Ideas

*Methods to Build Financial Freedom and Demolish Financial Stress*

By Adam Torbert

# Table of Contents

# BONUS!

Click here for instant access

As a simple "Thank you", I am glad to offer you the opportunity to gain complete access to an exclusive service which will send you valuable information which can additionally improve and strengthen your financial freedom. Along with that, you will be among the first people who will know when the upcoming books about making money will be available to help people. Free lifetime access to this exclusive service can be yours by simply following the link above.

# CHAPTER ONE: INTRODUCTION TO PASSIVE INCOME

How would your life look if you had some extra money? Do you want to make money the way the rich do? If your answer is yes and it should be, I'll help you out by sharing a secret: yes, you can make money like the rich. Yes, you can always make some extra cash for yourself. But the secret isn't aiming for the next promotion, working an extra ten hours per day, or aspiring to be the next chief medical director.

The secret to making more money for yourself is to seek out ways where your skills and money work for you "passively," meaning you put the systems in place and let them carry on without constant work being required on your part. To make money like the rich, you have to put strategies in place where you make money even while you are sleeping. That's a time-tested and trusted secret of building financial freedom. To build financial freedom and end financial stress, you need to know methods that will accomplish that for you. All you need are passive income ideas.

## What is passive income?

Passive income refers to the kind of money you earn without continual active involvement and

time commitment. Passive income ideas generate money for you on the go, whether you are directly engaged in an enterprise or are asleep. The goal is that while you are traveling, enjoying your holidays, and doing other things, your money will keep coming in which simply would not be possible if you followed the traditional route.

Passive income methods are "do and forget" systems to a point. You only have to set them up at the initial stage and then leave them to run themselves. Passive income gives you time to concentrate on other projects which can provide even more of the already mentioned benefits.

# Misconceptions about Passive income

People have misconceptions about passive income as with many other things. You need to know about those so that you do not make mistakes on your journey to building lasting wealth. You should act smartly and learn from the mistakes of others so that you don't have to commit mistakes. Here, I will be showing you what passive income is not and what you should unlearn before you proceed.

### *Misconception 1: Money you receive as a gift is passive income*

Some people regard passive income as money they receive as a gift. However, passive income is not the money your loved ones, friends, or other occasional benefactors send you. A gift is something that is received once in a while. Passive income is something that should generate income for you continuously over the course of time.

## *Misconception 2: Passive income means "no work"*

Making money through passive income ideas does not mean you won't work as nice as that may sound. All money-making ventures involve some level of work. However, passive income creation involves short-term work. After the initial stages, you wont have to work long or hard to make money with passive income methods even though some amount of involvement will still be necessary to keep things up and running.

## *Misconception 3: Passive income doesn't require commitment*

Another general misconception is that passive income requires zero commitment. Passive income actually requires a long-term commitment, starting with an upfront commitment in the initial set-up stages. Then you have to commit to continually investing in yourself, putting in the necessary time and delaying instant gratification until the systems are in place. That is generally some good life advice about always aiming for better and being willing to sacrifice short-term pleasure so that your future could be ten times better and more pleasant.

# Features of passive income

1. Less reliance on a nine-to-five job.
2. More freedom to manage your time
3. The opportunity to develop new ideas and sources of making money
4. Full control of your income level
5. Control of your destiny

# Why you should consider passive income today

I don't just want to tell you about passive income ideas in this book as it's way too easy to stop just at that. I also want you to take proactive measures in building wealth for yourself and putting an end to financial stress by showing you the clear reasons why you should consider passive income ideas. Once you internalize these reasons you will not want to go back to the old ways.

Beyond the fantastic feeling of receiving regular cash deposits without active work, passive income provides great benefits that will make you consider it an indispensable tool for creating wealth and gaining financial freedom.

### 1. Improved Financial Security

Despite how great your yearly job performance assessments may usually be, it can be difficult to know exactly what's going to happen at your day job. Maybe your organization hits a rough patch and the company needs to downsize. Maybe they can't give you a long-expected raise or they need to cut your benefits package. Maybe your boss had a bad day and your evaluation wasn't as stellar as it typically is. All of these situations are not something that has to do with how well you do your job which is actually the only thing you do have control over at your job. Unfortunately, your employer has full control of all such situations. Passive income helps put you in control so that you can be the one calling the shots.

Developing different methods of passive income helps diversify your cash streams as having only one stream of income these days is one of the riskiest strategies you can rely on. It creates assets you can easily control. The more passive income you have coming in, the safer you'll feel in case something does happen at your regular job. The same way you don't invest all your money in just one stock, you also shouldn't depend on earnings from one place alone. The principles are the same even though the situations are different.

## 2. Freedom to manage your own time

Passive income greatly increases the amount of time in the day for you. I quickly realized that people working such jobs can't be happy with the amount of free time they have and with money which they

are earning. Instead of being bound by the eight-hour, Monday-Friday workday, you can retain that job while also benefitting from the added advantages and money generated by your passive income ideas. The other option that will also be open to you is to work a part-time job instead which will probably end up being more fun than the usual corporate grind. You can also rely on your passive income entirely if you feel that you reached that level. Furthermore, if you have disciplined spending habits, passive income allows you to save up, giving you even more financial freedom. Financial intelligence is way beyond the scope of this book, but all that I will say on that topic is that nothing you can buy with money will make you as happy as financial freedom. Put the money from your passive income ideas as investments into new methods of generating and watch your active workforce of dollars grow!

### 3.  A sure road to financial freedom

If you won the lottery this weekend, would you plan to go to work on Monday? Is your job a picture of your passions, or just a way to a paycheck? Many of us, whether we like our jobs or not, would love the extra time with family, to travel, or to pursue hobbies, rather than spending all our time working to fulfill other people's dreams. Individuals who are committed to passive income can eventually buy themselves that freedom.

Remember what I said earlier about commitment? It generally takes planning and some years of developing your passive income streams before you can leave your full-time job. Everyone wants the magic key to immediate escape, but that commitment is important. Important thing is to know the fundamentals so that you can take action and learn from mistakes. Waiting for the magic pill or some missing strategy is the easiest way to waste time. And once your passive income surpasses your expenses, your day job becomes a choice, not a requirement. And isn't that what the attraction of financial freedom is all about? Not the yachts or the fancy cars, but the freedom?

# How to achieve Passive Income

There are hundreds of means for acquiring passive income. You can decide to sell crafts on Etsy, invest in the stock market, sell eBooks or print books online, invest in rental properties, sell your photographs, etc.! The key to getting started in passive income is to know what inspires you. Developing your passive income ideas takes work, and it helps if you focus on things you already love. It is important to choose one thing at a time so that you don't get shiny object syndrome and become a dabbler. Once you determine what you intend to focus on, decide on how much time you will devote to developing that particular passive income idea, set specific goals, and stick to them. Here are some simple ways to assist you in accomplishing your passive income idea.

### 1. Know what your skills and aspirations are

We all have gifts and different talents that we can use to help us develop sources of passive income. Think about what you would do with your time if you didn't have to constantly work and could chase your passion! If you're having doubts about whether you have the ability to create passive income streams, consider the individuals who make hundreds and thousands of dollars monthly in advertisements from *YouTube* videos of themselves playing video games. It never ceases to amaze me how many ways of making money are available these days.

## 2. Change your thought about Passive Income Vs. Active Income

Our educational system and our parents are fundamentally teaching us how to work for active income. We plan for the money. When we charge added money, individuals will tell us to get a part-time job, not to

build a business. So, already you've begun this journey of discovering your passion, you'll need to think in a new way to break off such a thought pattern. For instance, if your talent is playing the guitar, don't begin a business teaching guitar from your home. That's an active income idea, where you'll constantly be working, doing the teaching. You should focus more on creating product instead of services. Think about creating an online lesson or developing a *YouTube* channel with ad revenue. These are passive-income-generating ideas where you do the initial work and plan once, not over and over. Then, you sit back, relax, and earn money monthly or even daily.

### 3. Set Goals you can achieve

Passive income isn't an overnight journey. As I've stated before, you'll need an initial plan and will have to set realistic goals, then work toward those in a disciplined, organized fashion. You can begin by setting a target of $100 monthly, generated from passive income ideas, and work up from there. Even aiming to earn $10 initially can be a reasonable goal so that you can actually prove if your money making ideas produces results. It's important to reiterate that building wealth and gaining financial freedom through passive income is a journey, not a sprint.

### 4. Have a time frame to test your passive income idea

You should understand that not every venture you try will succeed. It will take time to determine if the passive income ideas you want to try will be successes or failures. Maybe you created an amazing product on Etsy, but no one buys it. It could be because you're a new agent who hasn't spelled out your SEO (search engine optimization) and marketing strategies to help increase sales. But it could also be, frankly, that no one wants your product. Just because you think it's amazing doesn't mean everybody else does.

Either way, before you begin your venture, know how much time and effort you're going to invest before you decide whether a particular passive income idea is a success or not. Six months? A year? When I started out with an idea for earning passive income by publishing books, I decided to treat it like a business for a complete year before I decided whether it was an effective revenue stream or was just a hobby. Time will determine where you will end up with each passive income idea in the long run. You should also try to seek out people that are successful in what you are trying to accomplish and learn from them.

## 5. Deal with the fear of spending money

The old saying "you need to spend money to make money" holds some truth. If you want your passive income streams to come in the form of dividends from stock market investments or rental fees from real estate properties, you'll need some money to start. But in today's innovative age, there are all kinds of opportunities that require little to no capital investment. Even before this time, some of the most popular brands in the world were created with less than $1000 initially invested. No amount of money will help a poorly-created eBook sell better. However, sometimes investing money can help you to succeed, so long as you start with a business plan for every transaction. Always know how you will define success, so you know to recognize it when you see it. Over time, stop pursuing the avenues that aren't clearly adding to your passive income stem. You're in this to earn money, not to spend it.

-I hope you are enjoying the book so far and that you are finding it helpful. If you wish to share your thoughts about the book so far, then you can do so by leaving a review on Amazon page.

# CHAPTER TWO: SELF-PUBLISHING

# BOOKS

If you love writing, self-publishing and selling eBooks, this is a passive income idea you can consider to build wealth and create financial independence for yourself.

One of the great things that happens after you publish an eBook is that, once you've successfully written and published, it has the potential to keep generating income for many years. In this case, you have pretty much created an asset for yourself. Once you have an eBook written, then you can also create a paperback version and an audiobook version of the same book. Audiobook sales are something that keeps on increasing in these times so it's certainly not something to overlook. All you need to do is to sit back and relax while income through royalties keeps arriving. To make money and build wealth through this passive income idea, you don't necessarily need to be a prolific writer with many books on similar topics in different niches. The secret of many successful self-published authors is to hire a writing company or a freelance ghostwriter to have the book written for them.

Many authors have gained financial independence through this singular passive income idea. They have published books in different sectors of human needs and, as a result, are now making money for themselves on a daily basis, without much active involvement in this venture. Steve Scott, a renowned publisher, made $40,000 to $50,000 monthly through his books in 2014. He only had books in two niches—Internet marketing and habits which are really hot topics.

## Categories of eBook writing

eBook writing can be classified into two broad categories:

- Fiction
- Nonfiction

Making money passively through published books is not just about-fiction books. I have friends who earn a steady amount of money writing and publishing fiction books. The potential for passive income through eBook publishing is massive as there is a broad worldwide market for your books in different niches. All that is required is to find those niches and needs.

## Options for self-publishing

There are three ways you can go about making passive income through self-publishing. Publishing books generally takes three forms:

- eBooks
- Print on Demand Books

- Audiobooks

Irrespective of the form or nature your book takes, it is important to know that you are going to need to put in the time and work upfront to succeed in this passive income idea. The upfront work will involve writing the books, editing and proofreading, designing covers, uploading the books to various online store platforms, and marketing them. If you aim at building wealth through the passive income idea of self-publishing, you have to put in the time to establish that framework. Like many things, the more you spend time with this process, the easier it will be and you will be able to put books out there sooner and sooner.

# Platforms to use in making money through book publishing

You will make use of online platforms to showcase your books to the world. There are various platforms you can use to self-publish your books and it would be a real shame not to take advantage of them. These platforms are free to join. All you need to do is to create an account with them, stick to their policies, publish your books on them, do little to no marketing, and royalties will come in on a monthly basis. Some of these platforms are:

- Amazon KDP

- Click Bank

- Audible (audio versions of your published eBooks)

- Smash words

- Barnes & Noble

- Draft2Digital

Publishing books is a great way of earning residual income month after month, even year after year. Technology has even made this passive income idea a lot easier and attractive as you can do it by yourself.

# Market Research for Self-Publishing Books

As an author or soon-to-be author, there is a need for you to do your homework and to do thorough market research on the genres that are highly sought after and which will be profitable to you in the long run. Doing market research helps you to invest and focus on ever-green niches that will add real revenue to your pocket thanks to their potential. New niches

are constantly popping up so being the early bird is something that can secure your position in a niche. Rather than gambling and experimenting with several niches, looking for the one that will pay off, market research will eliminate those hurdles and jumpstart you on your way to the real deal.

In conducting market research for profitable genres:

### 1. Look for similar best-selling titles

When you look for similar best-selling titles, the goal is to research the area of the market you want to publish your books in. Search for books written by authors within your genre. As a new author, you can also find relevant related book titles by new authors who have two or three books in print. Then, you can use an Excel sheet to compare the book titles and their contents. With this, you will be able to do deeper market research. It all comes down to noticing the keywords and the topics that people are searching for.

One good way to easily find comparable titles is to go through Amazon's search column and look for books with related keywords. For instance, if you intend to write a book on prosperity, go to Amazon.com and type "prosperity books." You should also use Amazon's autofill feature to see what people are searching for in relation to a certain keyword.

Another way to find related titles is to take a look at Amazon's best-sellers lists. You can do this by going to Amazon's Kindle store, going to the related category, and scrolling down to the best-sellers list in that chosen category. With Amazon's category search, you instruct Amazon on the bookshelf upon which your book will be placed for sale. The best approach for a beginner is to go deep into pretty specific niches and to find keywords that aren't too competitive and to then branch out from there.

## 2. Do an analysis of the book covers of your competitors

This is another great guideline. A book's cover is an important part of its branding. It helps to determine sales to a large extent. You may know of a proverb which says that you shouldn't judge a book by its cover, but in the world of selling books, you can be certain that people will judge your book by the cover. When you make your book cover look like those of your competitors, you are giving yourself an advantage in enticing readers to click on your book and look through some sample pages. This can turn into sales instantly. The book covers help to predict the type of books readers want to devour. In deciding book covers for your market, take note of these tips:

a) The various colors used in similar book covers

b) The fonts and sizes used

c) The size of the text and its placement

d) The emotions that the book covers evoke

e) The types of images used

Ensure that your book stands out among the other books in the category in which it is placed, especially if all the book covers look more or less the same. Remember the best elements from the covers of your competition and still try to be unique in some way. You must understand that people buy books based on emotions. This is a truly established fact, especially for non-fiction books. So, use that fact to your advantage and don't miss any opportunity to convert visitors to readers and book buyers when they first come in contact with your writing via your book covers.

### 3. Analyze the titles of competitors' books

In conducting market research for profitable genres for your book, analyzing the titles of similar books is very important. Word of mouth is a big determinant for why people buy books today. Hence, to capitalize on this, your book titles should be:

#### a) Memorable
Make your book title very easy for people to remember so they'll tell friends about it.

#### b) Repeatable
Repeat the book title in several parts of the book. Make sure it's clear, visible, and not confusing.

#### c) Searchable
After you have created your book in such a way that it is memorable and repeatable, also make sure it's easily searchable. Ensure it's unique with a unique title that can increase its ranking in search engines and Amazon search results.

# Websites that can be of help when you are conducting market research

While conducting suitable market research for your self-published book, you need to pay close attention to best-seller lists on reputable websites and book blogs. Studying these websites can only help your book sales. Such websites include:

1. Amazon Kindle
2. Barnes & Noble
3. Kobo Store
4. Apple iBook

These websites provide details of the best-selling books in each category and will help you decide what genre to pursue.

# Differences in conducting market research for fiction and non-fiction books

There are not many differences in conducting market research for fiction and non-fiction books. Whatever genre you select, research is essential to your success in your book publishing ventures.

One vital distinction that does exist between market research for fiction books and non-fiction books is the type of readers and the size of the audience. Types of readers and the size of the audience are quite different for fiction and non-fiction.

*What are the current trends for 2018?*

It's important, as an author, to study current market trends. While you can't guarantee that a specific genre will do well for you, you'll nevertheless give yourself an advantage by researching what genres are currently selling the best. Doing a bit more work in the beginning will mean that you will have to do less work in the future. Here are the lists of genres that have the best-selling books:

A) Fiction
  1. Romance
  2. Mystery and thriller
  3. Crime

B) Non-Fiction
  1. Self-Help
  2. Inspirational/Motivational
  3. Computers
  4. Business
  5. Religion

# Marketing Your Self-Published Book

When an author finishes writing a long-awaited book, it's almost always an exciting time. But that excitement isn't the end. In spreading the word about your newly-published book, you have to research ways to market it which will drive huge sales from the book and therefore produce more revenues for you. There are plenty of quality authors who, unfortunately, don't know how to market their books so their message ends up in obscurity.

So how do you accomplish that kind of marketing, exactly? Your book is on the market and the word is out that you're a great writer, but how do you build upon that? It's a definite challenge. The following list contains time-tested and trusted strategies and tips for marketing your book and increasing your sales. Here are the strategies to implement to increase the reach of your newly published book:

### 1. Using a freebie launch strategy

This strategy is very powerful and is guaranteed to increase the market awareness of your book. Self-publishing companies like Amazon KDP offer a free five-day promotional offer that allows authors to give out their book for free for a set period. With this, you make your book easily accessible to readers, potentially bringing in more future sales. There is no competing with free. It is worth mentioning that free eBooks on Amazon can be a good source of information for anything that may concern you about self-publishing business.

### 2. Facebook promotion

With Facebook advertisements and promotions, you can easily increase awareness of your newly self-published book in the market. One of the great aspects of marketing your book usingFacebook Ads is that the ads are niche targeted. Facebook is also an effective method for promoting a book freebie offer.

### 3. Reducing price

Another good way to increase market awareness of your newly self-published book is to reduce its initial price. Who doesn't love a discount, right? Some self-publishing platforms have a feature that enables authors to reduce the price of their books so that readers are drawn in to make immediate and repeated purchases. With this marketing strategy, you are on your way to making more sales as a result of increased awareness. There are features that show how long the discount will last which will give an impression that the potential readers should take action immediately. One interesting way to set price is to set a price a bit lower than you intended. If you were planning to price your eBook at $2,99, then what you should consider is setting it at $2,87 or something similar because it's been proven that such approach can more likely lead to a sale.

# Using Goodreads To Promote Your Book

Goodreads is a fantastic online platform that has become a favorite among authors to promote and market their self-published books. With a whopping 20 million active users, it is a social network that provides a platform for authors to meet readers and promote their books. In using Goodreads as a platform to market your books, here are the steps to take:

### 1. Get an author page set up

The first thing you need to do is to set up an author page. This is the most important step to connect with readers as it provides details about yourself, your book, and allows readers to learn about who you are, what you're writing, and also what you're reading. It will get you more exposure and more potential sales.

### 2. Get your books listed on Listopia

Ensure you list your books on Listopia. This allows you to place your book in the right genre, which makes it easier for buyers to add to a shopping cart. The fewer steps and potential complications there are, the better.

### 3. Get a little advertising done

This strategy is optional if you don't have the funds. But it helps a lot in the long run as Goodreads helps to target ready-to-buy readers. The cost is affordable—$0.15 per click. If you do the advertising right, then you won't have to worry about the cost because it will seem like you are getting free money. What is great about per click ads is the fact that you don't spend any money until someone clicks on your ad. You may need to do a bit of experimenting with cost per click in order to optimize this.

### 4. Offer free book giveaways

This is another powerful tip to market your self-published books on Goodreads as most readers enjoy freebies and frequently visit the free book giveaway section. This strategy will help to increase awareness and will generate book reviews. It is possible on some platforms such as Amazon to offer a free eBook if the paperback version of a book is purchased which is very neat.

### 5. Get your blog connected to your Goodreads author page.

Goodreads emails your fans about updates to your blog. So, whenever a new blog post is updated, your fans can connect with you. This way, you help to keep your fans following you, which can end up in a conversion to sales.

# Increasing Your Book's Visibility on Amazon

Amazon undoubtedly offers the largest platform for self-publishing in the world via its Kindle Publishing Direct (KDP) platform. Buyers and readers find many authors on Amazon KDP. But most are still faced with the problem of properly marketing their self-published books. A key factor is the book's visibility on KDP. To help increase the visibility of your book on Amazon:

1. Ensure your book, title, book's description, and search keywords are in line with the most recently searched items on Amazon. This first step is the most important one because nothing else will matter if the book itself is not of quality.

2. Politely ask for book reviews from readers. You can do this by simply including a note at the end of your book advertising free downloads and paid periods.

3. Try paid ads. These are an inarguably good way to increase your book's visibility on Amazon. Set aside a little amount of money for this purpose and in the long run, it will pay off well. Amazon ads are a pretty affordable option compared to some others like Facebook ads or Adwords.

4. You can also use your website. If you have a website/blog with a huge following, you can always redirect buyers and customers to your Amazon author page and book links. With this, your book's visibility will increase

5. Do email marketing. The email marketing feature is very important for increasing your book's visibility on Amazon. With email marketing, you can reach millions of readers and make them aware of your Amazon bookstore. You can also remind your current subscribers of what you're up to via emails. Most popular options for email marketing are Aweber and MailChimp.

# CHAPTER THREE: AFFILIATE

# MARKETING

Affiliate marketing has the potential for great profits. To succeed, however, you'll need to shift your mind to an Internet mentality. You cannot make any good progress in the digital age unless you move away from the old-fashioned way. Realize that the world is changing every day and that most restrictions that you thought existed are simply not around anymore.

Affiliate marketing is a business strategy that gives you the opportunity to advertise and sell other people's products online. There are many companies which offer great opportunities for affiliate programs. For instance, Amazon has a lot of things to offer in terms of sales of products. It is easy and cheap to start affiliate marketing and you can build a successful career. However, not everyone is making a lot of money in this business, so you need to have that in the back of your mind. Either way, using affiliate marketing to at least supplement your income is still recommended and over time it may grow into something that can't be ignored.

# Good Things About Affiliate Marketing

- You don't need a huge amount of capital to start out, unlike other capital-intensive businesses.

- There's absolutely no need for employing staff, paying for space, or storing products in a storehouse. Your online presence is all that is needed. It's as cost friendly as it gets.

- Affiliate marketing can be conducted from any location as long as you have a good laptop and a strong Internet connection. It is one of those beauties of living in a digital age.

- You don't use your money in affiliate marketing like you do in your usual job. You are only acting as a middleman in the whole transaction.

- You may not even have to be the one to deliver the products to your customers' home or shops. Vendors from the companies you are affiliated with will do that for you. It is as passive as passive income can get.

- The companies you are affiliated with will provide customer service so that's one thing less you have to worry about.

- Automation makes it possible for you to earn while you are asleep as long as your advertisement and content are online which isn't going away any time soon.

## The Downside of Affiliate Marketing

There are also downsides to affiliate marketing.

- Affiliate marketing looks good only if you are doing well in it. People who feel it isn't worth it are those who are not successful. You must work and make sales before you are paid at the end of the month.

- You need to learn affiliate marketing before you can be good at it. Don't jump into it until you know what it's all about. Things may get tough sometimes, but that is usual in life.

- You may spend time promoting what will not sell, so make sure you get the right products early in your business. Know what your customers are looking for.

- If you have a full-time business, it may clash with affiliate marketing, so use your time wisely. You may not see the profits immediately when you begin affiliate marketing. There will be a time of struggle, but, as you know, success is for those who never quit. Most ventures that you undertake will not yield immediate benefits, but those who can be patient and delay gratification do tend to be rewarded.

# Choosing the Best Affiliate Program

There are many affiliate programs to choose from, so initially choose the programs that are free, if you can. This way you can experiment while minimizing your risks. There is a lot of free training available and you should take advantage of that instead of spending your money on fees.

Different programs have dissimilar pay times. Some pay monthly, others weekly, or even biweekly. Choose the payment plan that you feel suits you best. Find out how much traffic a program allows you to generate before you are given a commission and make a choice based on that.

Check whether the company only pays a commission and doesn't include hits and impressions. Normally, hits and impressions should be paid, so find out what you stand to gain in the business, especially if the affiliate made provision for low sales in the hit ratio.

Be aware of the reputation of the online retailer you are doing business with to be sure it is a genuine business. It's all about providing a quality product or service in the end. Get familiar with the products they offer and be aware of how much the average price is.

Look out for the number of tiers the affiliate has. Two-tier programs pay you for the hard work plus the usual commission, while one tier only pays commission and nothing more.

# Great Ways to Boost Your Affiliate Commission

Now, let's get down to real business. Your purpose for passive income is to make money that will last for a long time or keep growing. Yes, every one of us has such a dream and you know what? You can double or even triple your income in affiliate marketing. Here's how you do it.

### *Promote Only the Best Program and Products*

Nothing pays more than getting the program that will give you the highest kind of profits. Since you are doing business, choose affiliate programs with the highest commission. Only quality products can stand the test of time and make you money in the long run. Good businessmen and women go for the most profitable business. Think like a seasoned business person. Good businessmen and women go for the most profitable business. You have to think like a seasoned business person to be successful in business.

### *Places where you can sign up as an affiliate marketer*

For you to find affiliate offers to promote, you must sign up on affiliate marketing websites. Luckily and obviously, businesses are more than happy to spread the word about their products.

There are many platforms online where you can sign up as an affiliate marketer. These platforms give you access to products which you can promote and use to earn commissions for yourself. Some of the popular affiliate marketing platforms are:

1) Clickbank

2) JVZoo

3) Commission Junction

4) Amazon

5) ShareASale

6) Warrior Plus

7) Click Booth

8) eBayPartner Network

9) Affiliate.com

10) Market Health

# CHAPTER FOUR: REAL ESTATE

# INVESTMENT

Real estate investment is another time-tested way you can earn long-term passive income for yourself. Value of real estate tends to go up with time which are the best forms of investment. I will share with you some tips and strategies you can implement to make residual income from real estate.

# 7 Secrets for Turning Real Estate into Real Passive Income

Selling high after buying low has always been the recommended tip for achieving success in real estate and in many other areas. Though this time-tested secret is true, it is not the way to make it big in the world of real estate. The real estate industry is known to have produced many multi-billionaires and is therefore considered one of the easiest ways to make money. Thus, the real estate industry can be your way towards making a fortune for yourself. We'll look at seven secrets of how with little or no money, you can easily turn the real estate market into a recurring passive income stream.

## 1. Begin on a small scale

Many individuals enter the real estate industry as full-time real estate businessmen or as part-time real estate dealers in combination with other businesses. I am a part-time real estate investor with interests in other business concerns. You can do the same. All you have to do is to maintain a business or job that brings in a regular cash flow for you and you can then diversify some of your income into real estate investments on a part-time basis.

If you are considering investing in real estate or you are a newcomer, it is always advisable to start on a small scale by using some of your money. As you start small, you will safely learn how to maximize profits and take advantage of deals. Few people in real estate have ever had an ultra-successful very first deal. You have to learn daily about building networks, read the fine print in contracts, and develop a good eye for great deals. All these can be obtained through experience.

One of the beauties of real estate investment is that you can learn all that needs to be learned even as you start small. You can start off by purchasing cheap properties around you such as single-unit homes, multiple-unit homes, or small business properties, then renovate them and flip them for sale at increased prices. It just involves a commitment.

## 2. Think big

Anyone, especially newcomers, can easily give up on real estate investment as a result of lack of funds. But the truth is that what matters in any real estate investment is the deal and not the budget. It is therefore advisable that you pursue the deal and ensure you get it, irrespective of how much you have.

## 3. Learn first and then earn

Education is very important. In becoming a successful real estate investor, the importance of education cannot be overemphasized. Nothing can take the place of information in the world of real estate. It is therefore important that before you think of investing in real estate, you obtain the right knowledge. As important as education is in the real estate industry, however, do not spend much money on seminars, workshops, and coaches. Do not be misled with the common notion that an expensive education is necessary. Information is available, plentiful, and inexpensive. So why spend more than necessary? Find it online, where it is readily available, or seek the expertise, knowledge, and experience of someone who has been successful in real estate.

You need to understand that holding onto assets is a fundamental way of creating wealth for yourself in real estate, as a shelter is a basic human need. By having a rental, you are in control of a business that will steadily produce income. Many young individuals want apartments close to the cities. It is therefore advisable that you buy houses in cities. Do not overinflate your budget. Part of the real estate business is expecting the unexpected and lowering your funds for increased returns and reduced risks. As a beginner, it is wise, to begin with one project at a time. Devise your model, modify it, and keep buying as the opportunities avail themselves. Continue with this system until you build a portfolio for yourself.

The tip for making a success out of your real estate business is to educate yourself. Get actively involved in the business; create value for clients and prospects. Cultivate the habit of taking positive, determined actions on a daily basis towards your goals. Go to meet-ups and seminars. Network and learn from others. When you are ready, and it's time to take decisive action on deals, act immediately.

## 4. Start now

There is no place for procrastination in the world of real estate. As a smart real estate investor, you have to act immediately on prospective good deals. In making a real fortune from real estate, I have personally used three strategies that have helped all along:

a) Buy properties at low rates. Property costs can be low

sometimes while demands are always consistent. When you buy properties and rent out, you create a passive income annually with returns of 10percent on the net worth. If you continue buying two or three cheap properties on a yearly basis, you will end up having twenty to thirty in ten years' time.

b) Flip up. All you need to do is to purchase a house that requires a little renovation at a great deal, live in it for a short time, and then flip it at an increased value for sale. When you do this consistently for a space of ten years, you will generate a great amount of money for yourself. You can then decide to buy your own house or reinvest in properties for rental purposes.

c) Enter a joint venture when necessary. You can make a joint venture deal with someone who has the money but lacks the eye to spot an opportunity in real estate. Look for a juicy deal and seal the contractual agreement while leaving the financial approval to be done within a framework of thirty days. Then get an investor to partner with and split the revenue into an agreed percentage. You can easily get a joint venture partner, but ensure you get the right one.

## 5. Profit comes in the deal

The profits in real estate only come through deals. Follow through quickly on good deals after you have done your thorough investigation and assessment monitoring. When you take a short time to seize on potential real estate deals, you not only position yourself to gain maximum profits, but you also bring minimum possible risks to the table and lessen the initial amount of money invested.

Before sealing a deal, ensure that you have a solid team of advisors and have followed your business plan. In maximizing profits, ensure you have an exit strategy so that when the winds are against you, there won't be much to lose in your investments. It is essential that you know the distinction between buying, selling, and trading. Your success in the real estate market is not solely based on your buying of property but on what you do with the property. The recommended strategy is to hold onto commercial real estate property for an extended time while you trade on small residential properties via rentals.

## 6. Have a strong understanding of the economics and dynamics of real estate

The real estate market is one filled with good and bad deals. Deals that seem to look good and which are worthy of investment are the most common and easy ones. Buying a property and renting it to tenants is easy, but provides the lowest returns on investment. You can easily find the most lucrative deals and opportunities in real estate. They are the ones you can spot and create. There is no better time to flip houses than now as there are low-interest rates and a high level of consumer confidence.

## 7. Find a mentor

I cannot overemphasize the importance of finding a mentor in the real estate business as they play a great role in your success. Mentors are there to teach, guide and lead you towards making maximum profits in real estate. Having a good mentor in a real estate business is a good way to go. Do not overlook this strategy as it determines, to a large extent, the outcomes of your investment in real estate.

The real estate market is one with great successes and equally great pitfalls. Educating yourself through research, books, and articles will help, but that can't take the place of a mentor. The time will come when you are in the heat of a good deal, and then a mentor will be your only help.

# HELPFUL TIPS

## 1. Be determined

If your core motivation for venturing into real estate investment is to reap instant riches, then you might want to think again. There's really nothing like quick money or easy money. No investment guarantees instant riches. Any form of real estate investment you want to venture into, be it house flipping or property rentals, requires real work and therefore requires some strong level of determination. If you aren't the determined type, you might end up frustrated. But if, on the other hand, you are tenacious, success awaits you, especially if you diligently follow the other tips I will share. Other than a determination to become a successful real estate investor, you must have carefully defined realistic goals and plans.

## 2. Have Focus and Discipline

Yes, you need focus and discipline. Their place cannot be

underemphasized. You will need focus and discipline when it comes to aspects of adhering to your budget and sticking to a plan already set out.

## 3. Set goals

Real estate investment is a venture just as it is a journey. You need to ask yourself: What do I want to achieve? Why do I want to go into real estate investment? What do I want to accomplish? In other words, you need to establish your goals. Know what you want. Have a smartly defined and written goal as you venture into real estate investment. If you don't have a clearly defined goal, you will not know when you achieve your purpose. A goal in real estate investment will help you to keep pressing on despite little hurdles as it will motivate you to continue until you achieve what you want. When the odds are against you, and your chances of success are down, it is your goals that will keep you moving.

## 4. Research and act

As part of your journey to achieving success in real estate investment, you will be required to do some legwork, such as researching. You should be ready to move from one location to another gathering facts and information. Though there are endless resources and information you can easily find on the Internet, your investment in materials like books and attending seminars will also pay off as they will help in building your knowledge base about real estate investment. It will also be beneficial to network with seasoned investors so that you can pick their brains and get wise pieces of information and advice.

Research, undoubtedly, is a very important tip in the journey to success in the real estate business but no matter how voracious you are in your research, it will amount to nothing if you fail to put the knowledge acquired into practical use. It is very unfortunate that many individuals in real estate investment do their research, but then fail to act on the information gathered. They rarely take the necessary actions, thus, they aren't successful. It isn't enough to do good research; you must act immediately and make the right decisions.

## 5. Always leverage

In real estate investment, there are many things you can leverage to maximize your success such as your relationships with others, technology, other people's money, expertise, ideas, etc. You should determine one thing you can leverage that will help you accomplish your desired goal in real estate. It will help you fulfill the potential of your real estate investment.

# CHAPTER FIVE: DROPSHIPPING

## What Is Dropshipping?

Dropshipping is one of the forms of selling goods online—e-commerce. It is similar to e-commerce but different in that it involves the sales of products from other suppliers or manufacturers on their behalf through promotions from your  base and channeling the requests of consumers to the manufacturers. The manufacturers then deliver the requested products to the customers. People regard dropshipping as the easiest and most straightforward way to have an online store where you sell products to consumers and earn residual income for yourself. All you need to do is to set up your store. Then you wait and obtain residual earnings for many years.

Recently, the focus has moved to dropshipping as a cool idea to earn passive income. There has also been an increase in the number of drop shippers in the world. Don't miss out on this way of earning passive income!

# Why DropShip As A Passive Income Idea

There are reasons why the dropshipping aspect of e-commerce is gaining massive popularity. Many dropshippers in the world have capitalized on the ready market of hungry consumers in various niches to make residual income for themselves and build wealth, thereby gaining financial independence. This section presents the many reasons why you should consider dropshipping as a passive income idea. The reasons outlined below will help you to quickly join the ever-increasing list of dropshippers who are making passive money for themselves.

## 1. Availability of consumer products

Undoubtedly, products, especially consumer products, are readily available. You will rarely search for a particular consumer product without finding it as there are always manufacturers who are willing to supply your needs. The availability of consumer products is on the ground that there is a high request for them in wholesale quantities. A determinant that has made products to be available is the fact that they address the specific needs of consumers in various niches. It has led to an increase in the number of dropshippers who are building wealth for themselves. You can also join them.

## 2. Easy evaluation

One other reason you should join the list of individuals making passive income through dropshipping is that consumers can efficiently evaluate products without any limitations. This helps to increase consumer confidence and encourages buying products online. That increase in consumer confidence will result in the growth in revenue of drop shippers and also creates a zero-return possibility.

### 3.  The Options for Upselling

With dropshipping as a passive income idea, you have the opportunity to upsell. You can quickly turn a larger profit when you sell other products related to those you have sold. For example, drop shippers can sell tablets and then up-sell tablet covers to buyers.

### 4.  High demand

The global e-commerce market has grown exponentially as many individuals all over the world have come to embrace online shopping. Experts have predicted that the industry will keep growing. If you are looking for a profitable passive income, dropshipping is the right one to pursue. Drop shippers are ever increasing as unfilled niches are in high demand from consumers across the world.

# Platforms You Can Sign Up for as A DropShipper

There are several platforms you can sign up with as a drop-shipper to make residual income. These are:

1. Oberlo

2. Shopify

3. Doba

4. Salehoo

5. Alibaba

6. Worldwide Brands

7. Wholesale Central

8. Dropship Direct

9. Sunrise Wholesale

10. Wholesale2b

# 4 Elements of Achieving Success Using DropShipping As A Passive Income Idea

## 1. Value orientation

Nothing drives success in a business like value creation. To achieve dropshipping success, you must be a value-driven person. People always want to know the value they will get from your products. Where they cannot perceive any derivable value, they will purchase a product from someone else. In creating value to increase your residual income through as dropshipping, you need to:

1) Do all you can to make your customers keep coming back for your products—make sure they feel they're getting good value for their money

2) Provide customers with useful information, insights, and tips

3) Provide solutions for their needs and challenges

4) Make them feel better when they buy your products


## 2. A good niche

You cannot earn passive income if you don't concentrate on a particular niche. The niche you choose will determine your passive earnings. If you want dropshipping success, focus on a targeted niche. Concentrate your efforts on a particular niche, know the needs of the people there, and position yourself to provide the solutions better than anyone else.


## 3. Get your Marketing and SEO right

One thing that will determine dropshipping success is traffic. The right marketing and SEO are very important elements of your dropshipping success. Do not relegate them to the background. If you are skilled in marketing and SEO, use them to improve your chances of dropshipping success. If you are not skilled in those areas, outsource the work to professionals.

## 4. Outstanding service

To be successful in a passive income dropshipping venture, deliver outstanding service to your customers. Your reputation is at stake. Offering excellent and top-notch service will increase your dropshipping success rate and residual income.

# CHAPTER SIX: CREATING AN

# ONLINE COURSE

Creating an online course is another passive income idea. You can monetize your skills and earn passive income from them consistently. What skills do you have? What are you good at doing? Develop a passive stream of income around it. All you need to do is to create an online course for it in the form of videos and put these up for sale online.

Online courses may cover an exhaustive range of niches and subject areas such as the medical field, technology, astronomy, arts and crafts, and even the entertainment world, including music.

The use of videos on *YouTube,* for instance, enables people all over the world to get degrees and diplomas and other notable certification without necessarily having to learn within the four walls of a physical class. The beauty of this passive income idea is that participants can learn at their own pace while still being involved in other endeavors.

### *Platforms you can use to sell your online courses*

- Udemy

- Tutsplus

- Code Academy

- Teachable

- Thinkific

- Your own website

To start, write out a list of skills that you have or things that you are good at doing. Pick one and go with it. There are courses on just about anything and a ton of people willing to learn. This is a great opportunity since you only have to work at it in the beginning to get it up and running. Once this is done that's it! No more work needed and you have a course that sells online without your presence.

An online course you create today has great potential for providing you with residual income for life. Monetize your skills today. Create a stream of passive income for yourself. Sign up on these platforms to begin making a passive income from online courses you create.

# CHAPTER SEVEN: CREATE

# MOBILE APPS

Creating a mobile application is a passive income idea. The simple technique here is to discover a problem to be solved and create an app around it. Today, there a variety of apps in the technology market. Some solve complex problems such as mobile banking and airline ticketing. Others apps include ones for checking Body Mass Index (BMI), pregnancy tests, and apps for easy use of certain platforms such as Facebook,

Upwork, Amazon Kindle, etc.

Did you know that a few years ago, creating mobile apps cost hundreds or thousands of dollars? That was discouraging to individuals then. But now, things are easy. You can easily create apps by yourself and sell them on various online platforms like Google Play. If you are not skilled at mobile app development, you can outsource to a professional developer and pay a one-time fee to develop your mobile app.

You can make residual income for life from a single mobile app, so long as you sign up on platforms where you will be displayed to the global audience. When they purchase your app for use, you earn a royalty. This earning can keep increasing, thereby serving as a source of passive income for you.

This method of earning passive income is currently trending and will keep doing so for a long time to come. It is interesting to note that the skills needed to develop a mobile app can be learned without the need for engineering or programming background knowledge. They can be learned through online courses and even through simple *YouTube* videos.

This is a great way to earn passive income because once the app is up and running, and online for people to use, very minimal work is needed thereafter. Your app will be downloaded without your presence and it can generate a passive stream of income without any further work.

There are many ways to monetize your app even if you provide it as a free download. Some of the ways are to show ads in your app when someone clicks the ad you get paid. You can have in-app purchases or premium versions of your app.

However, you decide to monetize it, creating an app is a great way to generate passive income.

# CHAPTER EIGHT: BLOGGING

Blogging is probably one of the best ways to generate passive income online. Why? Because it allows you to connect and build an audience outside of any other platform. It also allows you to promote all your other passive income streams in one spot. It's one of the best ways to affiliate market products and services by writing reviews and reaching out to your following. You can also rank on search engines for your blog posts to get free organic traffic.

You can use your blog to promote your app, you can use it to promote your online course, your affiliate products or services, your e-commerce website, YouTube videos, and the list goes on. By driving traffic to your blog, you also help support all the other passive income streams, it becomes the center of all that you do and it's one of the best ways to build trust with your audience which will lead to more sales and more income.

A blog is the perfect middle point for all passive income. Although you have to be active in creating blog posts and content, it helps drive sales to all your other passive income streams. You can also outsource your blog content to other companies or freelancers to make it completely passive. Blogging is the perfect option to tie everything together, to build a brand, and build a following.

Another way blogging can lead to passive income is through paid advertising where others pay you to advertise their content on your site. The more traffic your blog has the more you can charge for ads on your pages. This only requires an initial setup for your pages for ad placement but once that is done there is nothing more to it. You will collect payment every week or month, however, the agreement is set up, and no further work is needed on your part.

You should use WordPress as it's the best blogging platform out there. WordPress makes it really simple to get your blog up and running without all the technical code to putting a website together. WordPress was originally designed with blogging in mind so it's built right into the platform.

Setting up a blog is simple, first, you need a domain for your website. Then, a hosting provider to host your website.

### *Domain name and hosting providers:*

- Namecheap

- GoDaddy

- Bluehost

Then, you need to install WordPress on your website. If you go with one of the hosting providers above, they have a one-click install for WordPress.

The best part about going with WordPress is you don't need to be a graphic designer to create a well-designed website. WordPress provides themes, both free and premium, that you can install on your site.

***Best spots to find themes:***

- WordPress official site

- Theme Forest

- Themify

WordPress also comes with 100s of plugins so you can add just about anything to your website without writing a single line of code. This option for customization makes things really fun. The plugin marketplace is built right in, making it very easy for you to add extra functionality to your blog.

Once you have all this setup, it's time to start working on your blog posts!

Remember, you can write them yourself or you can outsource it to a company or freelancer. The choice is yours!

# CONCLUSION

So, there you have it. Passive income ideas that will help to build financial freedom and demolish financial stress in your life and generally make your life better.

The idea of generating passive income sounds great but it doesn't mean you will do zero work. In building wealth for yourself and gaining financial freedom, you have to work for it. Passive income ideas make the process simple as you only have to work at the initial stage of setting up the venture. Then you wait and earn residual income to your accounts for years—even while you are sleeping or doing anything else.

I encourage you to begin your journey of building financial freedom today through the passive income ideas shared in this book. The sooner you start, the sooner you can reach your goals. Don't wait for the perfect moment or state of mind. Create streams of passive income for yourself today.

The best way to start is to choose one and stick with it. Gather additional information online about the topic and find out how to get started. Try to make sure that you don't get stuck on just gathering information and not taking any action. If you need to, don't be afraid to invest in a course to teach you the necessary skills. Make sure that the course creator is still doing the thing in the course so that you can be sure that the content of the course is up to date with current trends. Spend some time after work, an hour or two, on building it. If you can do this every day, time will quickly add up and before you know it, you will be generating income without you being physically present. But, the key here is to focus on one passive income stream, one idea, at a time. Put in 100% effort and have it earning you some passive income first before moving onto the next idea. Don't fall victim to shiny object syndrome.

It's life-changing stuff and can really supplement and add to your current income. Take action and be persistent and you will make it work!

I hope that you enjoyed reading through this content and that you are willing to provide feedback for the book by leaving a review at

Made in the USA
Columbia, SC
21 November 2018